The Lake District

Jean Patefield

COUNTRYSIDE BOOKS

NEWBURY BERKSHIRE

First published 2012
© Jean Patefield 2012

COUNTRYSIDE BOOKS
3 Catherine Road
Newbury, Berkshire

To view our complete range of books,
please visit us at
www.countrysidebooks.co.uk

ISBN 978 1 84674 286 6

Photographs and maps by the author

Designed by Peter Davies, Nautilus Design
Produced through MRM Associates Ltd., Reading
Printed by Information Press, Oxford

Contents

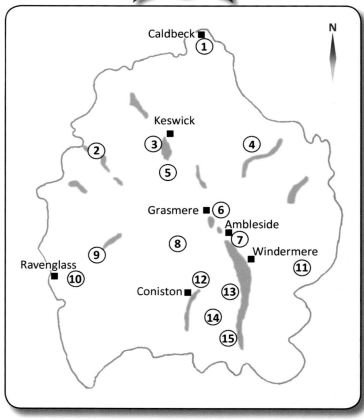

Area map showing location of the walks

Introduction

The Lake District is England's best loved walking area. It has cast its spell over visitors since the earliest days of tourism over 200 years ago. Thousands upon tens of thousands escape to its freedom and beauty every year and only constant effort by the National Park authorities and others such as the National Trust prevents it being loved to death. And yet there are many quiet corners where its peace can be enjoyed away from the crowds. It exerts its special charm at all times of the year and is never the same as the light and weather change. No corner of England has attracted so many writers and artists and it has inspired some of the best-loved poetry and prose.

The fifteen walks in this book are all between 2 and 6 miles and should be within the capacity of the average person. Some of the walks stick to the valleys and are fairly level. Others explore the hills and so involve some climbing. However, this presents no problem to the sensible walker who has three uphill gears: slowly, very slowly and admiring the view.

All the routes are on public rights of way, permissive paths or open fell and have been carefully checked. An Ordnance Survey map is useful for identifying the main features of views. The Explorer 1:25,000 (2½ inches to 1 mile) series are the best maps to use for walking. Sheets OL 4, 5, 6 and 7 cover the walks in this book. The grid reference of the starting point and the appropriate maps are given for each route.

Nowadays pubs are often the best places to eat out in England and all the ones recommended in this book offer good food and a warm welcome. Many of them serve beers offered by the many small breweries that have sprung up across the Lake District. The opening times, telephone number and web site address of each pub are included. The walks are complemented by the suggestion of a nearby place of interest you might like to visit to make a full and enjoyable day out.

The directions for the walks all start at the suggested pub.

Occasionally it is possible to use the pub car park. Do please remember to seek the landlord's permission first. However, many of the best-loved Lake District pubs featured in this book have tiny car parks or none at all so the landlord will not welcome you leaving your car and many have notices expressly forbidding this. In addition, these same pubs often have very limited or no street parking nearby. In such cases, it is more sensible to start the walk somewhere else where parking is available and visit the pub part way round the walk and this sometimes fits in better with the plans for the day too. There are details of this for walks where it is particularly necessary or appropriate.

Jean Patefield

Publisher's Note

We hope that you obtain considerable enjoyment from this book; great care has been taken in its preparation. However, changes of landlord and actual closures are sadly not uncommon. Likewise, although at the time of publication all routes followed public rights of way or permitted paths, diversion orders can be made and permissions withdrawn.

We cannot, of course, be held responsible for such diversion orders and any inaccuracies in the text which result from these or any other changes to the routes, nor any damage which might result from walkers trespassing on private property. We are anxious though that all details covering the walks and the pubs are kept up to date and would therefore welcome information from readers which would be relevant to future editions.

The simple sketch maps that accompany the walks in the book are based on notes made by the author whilst checking out the routes on the ground. For the benefit of a proper map, however, we do recommend that you purchase the relevant Ordnance Survey sheet covering your walk. The Ordnance Survey maps are widely available, especially through booksellers and local newsagents.

1 Hesket Newmarket

The Old Crown

This is a very easy and attractive walk at the northern fringe of the National Park, undeservedly overlooked by many visitors, and very quiet compared with the rest of the Lakes. It explores the valley carved by the Cald Beck and visits two interesting villages. The route starts in Hesket Newmarket whose market was new when its charter was granted in 1751. Today it is an attractive village, with many 18th-century buildings. The route

Distance – 4½ miles.

OS Explorer OL5 The English Lakes – North-eastern area. GR NY 341386.

Starting point The Old Crown, Hesket Newmarket. There is no car park at the pub but the village car park is about 100 yards away and there is also some parking round the village green.

How to get there From the A66 Penrith–Keswick road 8 miles east of Keswick take a minor road signed 'Mungrisdale and Caldbeck' and follow the signs to Caldbeck until you reach Hesket Newmarket. Hesket Newmarket is also signed from the B5305, Penrith–Wigton road.

Alternative To visit the pub part way round the walk, start in Caldbeck where there is a public car park (GR NY323399) to pick up the route at point 7. Caldbeck has a pub, the Oddfellows Arms (☎ 016974 78227), a Jennings house that serves food every lunchtime, and a couple of teashops.

leads through open country with wide views to the waterfalls at the Howk where the river surges through a ravine carved in the limestone, guarded by the romantic ruin of a bobbin mill. After visiting neighbouring Caldbeck, the birthplace and final resting place of the famous John Peel, we climb through woodland up the side of the valley to an excellent viewpoint with a vista of the Lake District fells before descending to the confluence of the Cald Beck and River Caldew at Watersmeet to follow the river back to the start.

THE PUB

The **Old Crown** in Hesket Newmarket is a unique pub that upholds the finest tradition of English inn-keeping: a warm, cosy, friendly pub, selling good food and tremendous beer, such as Skiddaw Special and Doris' 90th birthday Ale brewed at Hesket Newmarket Brewery behind the pub. Both the brewery and the pub are owned by local co-operatives to protect their future. Well-behaved dogs and children are welcome.

The pub is only open during the day on Friday, Saturday and Sunday, and Wednesday and Thursday in school holidays, serving food between noon and 2.30 pm. ☎ *01697 478288; www.theoldcrownpub.co.uk.*

1 Turn left out of the pub through **Hesket Newmarket**. As the main road bends right, bear left on a lane to the left of **Berkeley House**. Ignore a lane and path immediately on the left and walk along the lane, ignoring further paths on the left, for just over ½ mile to the first signed path on the right.

2 Turn right through a gate, signed 'Matthew Rudding ¼ mile'. Walk along the left-hand side of a meadow to a gate on the left, then head diagonally across the next field to bear left past the farm onto the farm drive. Walk along the drive and **Caldbeck** comes into view in the valley below.

3 At a lane turn right over the river. Immediately after the parish hall, bear left to a main road. Turn left for 100 yards.

4 Turn right through a wooden kissing gate, signed 'The Howk'. Walk along the right-hand side of a field to a second kissing gate and down some steps to a footbridge over the river.

5 Over the bridge, turn right up some steps. At the top, turn right again for 40 yards, then turn right again, down steps, to a riverside path. Follow this, passing the remains of a bobbin mill and an information board that tells you all about it. Keep ahead through a courtyard to emerge at a road junction.

The Lake District

6 Turn right for 75 yards, over the river yet again, then left on a signed path, now walking with the river on the left, into **Caldbeck**.

7 Cross the road and take a riverside path a few yards to the right, signed 'Church Terrace ¼ mile', to a surfaced cross path at the church. Turn left over the river, then turn right to continue in the same direction on the other side. Keep ahead through a gate as the road becomes a track and then a path. When the path forks just after a water treatment works, keep ahead through a gate rather than over the stile to the left and continue for 170 yards to another fork, shown by a waymark post.

8 Bear left on a rising path and follow this through woodland to a gate out of the woods. Keep ahead for another 100 yards.

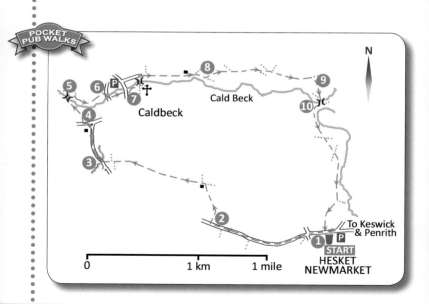

9 Turn right to a stile over a fence back into the wood. Follow the path steeply down to find a footbridge over the river.

10 Over the bridge, follow the path as it bears right to a gate. Through the gate, follow the path uphill along the left-hand side of a field. Towards the end of the field, bear left to a wooden kissing gate, then follow the waymarked path along the top of the slope to eventually reach a small gate into a field. (Note: The waymarked path is not as the right of way shown on the OS map.) Head across the field into **Hesket Newmarket**.

Place of interest nearby

Caldbeck church dates from 1142. Two legendary residents are buried in the churchyard. John Peel, the renowned huntsman, was born in Caldbeck in 1776 though he spent most of his life about six miles away at Ruthwaite. Mary Robinson, the Beauty of Buttermere, was the daughter of the landlord of the Fish Inn in Buttermere. She unwisely married a confidence trickster and bigamist, John Hatfield, posing as the Hon. Augustus Hope M.P. for Linlithgow. When he was caught, he was charged with defrauding the Post Office as he had been franking his own letters rather than with bigamy. The jury at Carlisle were reluctant to hang a man for fiddling the Post Office but were stirred by the fate of Mary, by then pregnant, and John Hatfield was hanged on 3 September 1803. The case caught the public imagination and several books and plays were written about the Beauty of Buttermere. She returned to her father's inn where she became quite a celebrity before marrying a farmer from near Caldbeck. Mary lived a long life and raised a large family before she was finally laid to rest in the churchyard.

2 Loweswater & Crummock Water

The Kirkstile Inn

Looking at the title of this walk, you might very reasonably assume that it visits two lakes – but not so. It starts at the eponymous village of Loweswater, with its famous ancient pub next to the church and wends its way to the shore of Crummock Water for a stroll by the lake. The route to and from the lake is a pleasing combination of woods and quiet field paths and tracks. On the outward leg there are superb views into the central fells, including a view down Crummock Water that rivals, if not surpasses, Britain's Favourite View (see Walk 9). On the return leg the views are more pastoral and include the very pretty lake, Loweswater itself.

Distance – 4 miles.

OS Explorer OL4 The English Lakes North-Western area. GR NY141209.

Starting point Kirkstile Inn, Loweswater village.

How to get there From the B5289, Buttermere–Cockermouth road, follow the signs to Loweswater. At a red telephone box, take a minor road to the Kirkstile Inn, next to the church.

Alternatives There is no other source of refreshment on this walk. If you wish to visit the Kirkstile Inn part way round the route, start at the car park for Lanthwaite Wood (GR NY149214) just north-east of the village and passed at point 4 and on the minor road from the B5289.

THE PUB

The **Kirkstile Inn** is a wonderful old pub housed in buildings that date back to the 16th century. The setting is beyond compare and the views can be enjoyed from the garden overlooked by a light, bright gallery and the dining room. In the main bar there is an open fire, welcome in less than clement Lake District weather. In the old days, of course, beer was brewed on the premises and this tradition was revived in 2003 when Loweswater Brewery was started at the Kirkstile. In 2009 production moved to Hawkshead when they took over Cumbrian Legendary Ales but the same beers are still produced, including the delicious and award-winning Loweswater Gold. In addition, they normally have at least one other Cumbrian real ale such as Yates bitter.

The food is just as good and at lunchtime there is a choice of sandwiches and baguettes or filled jacket potatoes, as well as some very tempting savoury suggestions such as black pudding and haggis balls with onion whisky marmalade. For those with

The Lake District

a more robust appetite, full meals are available, including Cumberland tatie pot, a lamb stew with black pudding, potatoes and vegetables.

Lunch is served between noon and 2 pm every day and food is available in the evenings between 6 pm and 9 pm. ☎ *01900 85219; www.kirkstile.com.*

1. Turn right out of the **Kirkstile Inn** car park then take the first left, past the church on the left.

2. At a road junction turn right along a signed path starting along a track. When the track ends at a house, keep ahead on a waymarked path to shortly reach a stile. Over the stile, turn left to walk across three fields, navigating from stile to stile, to a lane.

3. Turn left to a crossroads then turn right and walk along the road to the far side of a bridge.

4. Over the bridge turn right along a track signed 'Lanthwaite 1 mile', passing a car park on the right. Bear right at a fork. Keep

Crummock Water

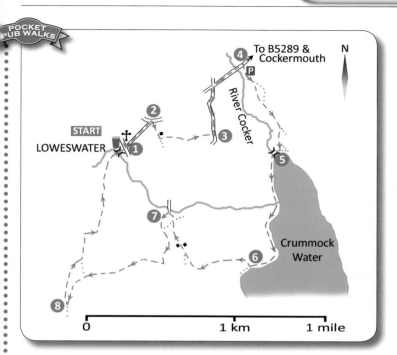

ahead as a track joins on the left then bear right again at two more forks to reach **Crummock Water** and a seat to admire the magnificent view down the lake.

5 Turn right to walk by the lake, crossing the **River Cocker** at a couple of footbridges and past the fish weir and pump house. Continue by the lake to reach a shingle beach bisected by a fence.

6 Before going through a gate in the fence, turn right away from the lake to walk with a wall on the left for about 50 yards. Go through a gate on the left and head up a field to another gate. As you climb, the

15

The Lake District

previously hidden end of **Crummock Water** comes into view. Keep ahead to a stile by a gate. Over the stile continue along what is now a track and press on past houses on the right and left, now between walls. Ignore the first track on the left and continue for 30 yards to a second, just where the track becomes surfaced.

7 Turn left, signed 'Ennerdale Water 4½ miles'. When the track ends, carry on ahead on a walled path to a gate and then up through woodland with a wall on the right. Stay on the path as it turns sharp right. The wall is eventually replaced by a fence and at this point there is a path down to a track. You can cut down here but it is steep and rough and it is easier to carry on beside the wood to meet a cross track.

8 Turn very sharp right and follow this path back to the inn.

Places of interest nearby

The nearest town to Loweswater is **Cockermouth**, so-named because it lies where the River Cocker, which drains Crummock Water, flows into the River Derwent. This charming small town is an enjoyable place to just wander, with many unique specialist shops. **Jennings Brewery** moved to Cockermouth in 1874 and tours are available which should be booked in advance, (☎ 0845 1297190; www.jenningsbrewery.co.uk. If you are more interested in history, **Wordsworth's birthplace** is fascinating. The poet was born there in 1770. After a chequered history, including being nearly knocked down to make way for a bus station in the 1930s, it is now in the care of the National Trust who have restored it to its 18th-century condition. ☎ 01900 820884; www.wordsworthhouse.org.uk

3 Around Swinside

The Farmers Arms

Swinside is the isolated hill that resembles a cork just pulled from the neck of the Newlands Valley. It is often overlooked and Wainwright failed to include it in his famous guide books to the Lake District fells. However, unlike many of its grander neighbours, Swinside is a Marilyn, which is defined as a hill with a drop of 492 ft on all sides. The term 'Marilyn' was coined as an ironic contrast to the designation Munro, used of a Scottish

The Lake District

Distance – 5 miles.

OS Explorer OL4 The English Lakes North-western area. GR NY 249237.

Starting point The Farmers Arms, Portinscale.

How to get there From the A66 west of Keswick, take a minor road signed 'Grange Newlands Portinscale' to Portinscale. The Farmers Arms is on the main road through the village on the left.

Alternatives The Farmers Arms dates from before the pre-eminence of the car and has very little parking of its own. There is some limited street parking nearby. An alternative is to use the parking place at Hawse End, GR NY246211. To find this, continue on the same road through Portinscale, bearing left at two junctions. When the road zig-zags, take a minor surfaced road on the right, which has a parking sign, to a parking area on the left. You would now start the walk at point 4, continuing along the lane. There is no other pub on the route but some of the hotels in Portinscale have a public bar.

mountain with a height of more than 3,000 ft. The land is privately-owned and there is no public footpath to the summit. It was much more highly regarded in the past when it was one of the seven 'stations' around Derwentwater visited by Victorian tourists. It was the custom then to turn one's back on the view and look at it in a convex mirror, a Claude glass, to better appreciate its artistic merit.

The circumnavigation of Swinside makes an interesting and varied walk in magnificent scenery. The route starts in Portinscale and explores the lovely woods on the west side of Derwentwater, heading straight for Catbells, the distinctive hill that overlooks the lake. On reaching its foot, the route turns aside to drop down into the valley to find the attractive Newlands Beck, before quiet lanes and field paths lead back to Portinscale.

THE PUB The **Farmers Arms** in Portinscale is a Lakeland village pub, which has a beer garden for warmer days. The lunchtime menu includes a choice of sandwiches, served with soup if you wish, as well as more substantial meals and some tempting puddings. A Jennings house, it serves the full range of their beers, including the intriguingly-named Cross Buttock bitter, which takes its name from a Cumbrian wrestling throw.

Food is served between noon and 2 pm, as well as in the evenings.
☎ *01768 772322; www.thefarmersarms.net.*

Turn left out of the **Farmers Arms** and walk out of the village, following the signs for **Grange and Newlands Valley**.

Some 40 yards after the turning to **Nichol End**, take a signed footpath on the left through woodland to a track. Continue in the same direction to the entrance to **Lingholm**, crossing the entrance drive. Take a path signed 'Catbells' next to the gate. Follow the path through woods and across parkland to a lane.

Cross the lane and continue in the same direction signed 'Catbells Newlands Valley', going uphill beside a wall on the right, to a second lane.

Turn left and then right along a tiny lane to **Skelgill Farm**. Go through a gate across the lane and continue between farm buildings. Walk along the surfaced farm lane down to a road.

Turn right for 300 yards to a public footpath on the left beside **Newlands Beck**, signed 'Braithwaite 1½ miles'. Follow the path

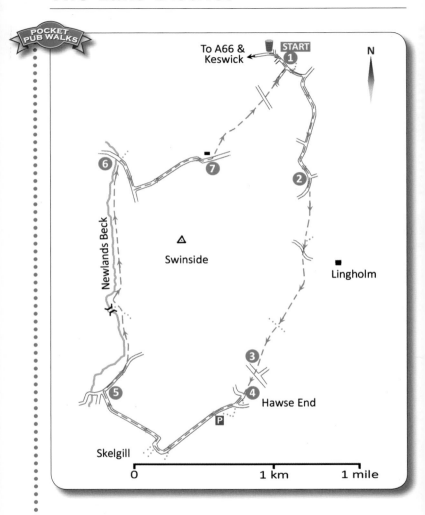

To A66 & Keswick

START
1

N

2

6

7

Newlands Beck

△
Swinside

Lingholm

3

4 Hawse End

5

P

Skelgill

0   1 km   1 mile

on the right-hand bank of the beck for about 1 mile, passing an attractive old bridge.

6) At a bridge carrying a minor road, turn right along the road for 300 yards and then turn left, signed 'Ullock ¼'.

7) Just after the last building, **Yew Tree Cottage**, turn left on a footpath, signed 'Portinscale Village ½ mile', through a small gate. Follow the clear path to a lane. Cross the lane and carry on in the same direction on a fenced path a few yards to the left. Keep ahead when this is shortly surfaced to a road. Turn left back to the **Farmers Arms**.

Place of interest nearby

Having exercised your body with a lovely walk, why not fascinate your mind with a visit to the **Puzzling Place** in Keswick, a unique optical illusion exhibition that is well worth a visit. Be amazed by sitting in a chair that glides on rollers uphill in the anti-gravity room, watch your companions grow and shrink in the Ames room and be intrigued by the interactive optical illusion exhibits, artwork and sculptures, as well as the hologram gallery. Even when you know what is going on, the effects are still amazing and make you wonder if you can ever believe your eyes again. The Puzzling Place is in the middle of Keswick but hidden away in Museum Square, just off the main road at the north end of the pedestrianised section, at the top of some stairs. There is a shop and a small area of puzzles that is free but entry to the main exhibition is reasonably priced. They are open every day during the school holidays and throughout the summer, just closing on Monday in winter. During January they are only open at the weekend. ☎ 017687 75102; www.puzzlingplace.co.uk.

The Royal Hotel

This walk combines all the elements that make the Lake District so special. It has woods, a minor summit to conquer, breathtaking views of Ullswater, and finishes with a visit to one of the Lakes' best-known beauty spots, Aira Force. It is a memorable sight – and sound – from the stone bridges above and below the falls as Aira Beck plunges some 70 ft vertically down a narrow rocky chasm into the pool beneath the lower bridge. The route also passes the upper falls of High Force, which drop some 35 ft and are also impressive, particularly when in spate.

Distance – 4½ miles.

OS Explorer OL5 The English Lakes North-eastern area. GR NY 393216.

Starting point The Royal Hotel, Dockray.

How to get there *The walk starts at Dockray, which is on the A5091 connecting the A66 with the A592. It is about a mile north of the junction with the A592. The Royal has a reasonable car park but if you are not intending to call in at the pub, there is a small area where you can park near the bridge.*

Alternative *If you wish to visit the Royal Hotel part way round the walk, start at the car park for Aira Force (National Trust, charge for non-members). Take the path out of the rear of the car park. Cross a footbridge on the right. When this path forks, bear left to walk with the river on the left, picking up the route at point 5.*

THE PUB The **Royal Hotel** at Dockray is a traditional country hotel that has developed from a former coaching inn where both Mary Queen of Scots and Wordsworth are reputed to have stayed. Walkers are welcome in the bar where Black Sheep, Jennings and a guest beer are served. In good weather you can enjoy your food and drink in the pleasant and extensive garden in a great setting. The bar menu ranges from tasty sandwiches to full meals, including some tempting puds such as summer fruit pudding with Chantilly cream when I visited.

Food is served between noon and 2 pm and from 6 pm all year. ☎ *017684 82356; www.the-royal-dockray.co.uk.*

The Lake District

1. Take a track opposite the **Royal Hotel** signed 'Aira Force and Ulcat Row'. Ignore a path on the left after the last building and continue, signed 'Gowbarrow Fell and Aira Force' to a gate in a wall.

2. Through the gate turn left on a permissive path, signed 'Gowbarrow Fell'. This reaches a gate in a wall after 90 yards and then continues uphill with a wall on the left. As you climb, there are superb views backwards (every excuse to stop and admire them) of the foot of **Ullswater** and **High Street**. **Helvellyn** gradually comes into view. Continue on the path as it swings right away from the wall to the trig point on the summit of **Gowbarrow Fell**.

Aira Force

3. After admiring the view, leave the summit by the same path. After a few yards turn right and follow the path downhill. (Note: the path directly from the trig point is very steep and awkward and joins the recommended path a short way down.) Continue on the clear path as it bends right to contour round the hillside and joins a path coming in from the left by a derelict shooting lodge. There are magnificent views over **Ullswater**, with a seat very well placed to admire them. The path gradually

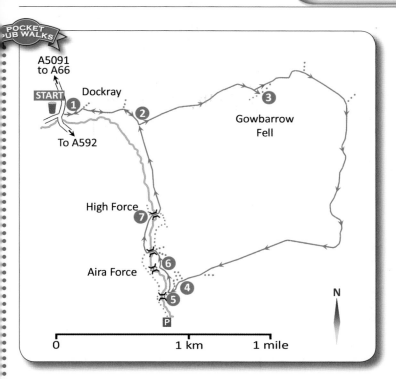

POCKET
PUB WALKS

A5091
to A66

START

Dockray

To A592

Gowbarrow
Fell

High Force

Aira Force

P

N

0   1 km   1 mile

descends to reach a fork about 1½ miles after passing the shooting lodge.

4 At the fork, take the left branch to keep ahead to a small gate in a fence. Ignore two paths on the right and continue until, within sight of the river, a path joins on the right.

5 Turn right along this path to walk above the river on the left, passing some steps on the right, to reach a stone bridge over the river with the best view of **Aira Force**.

The Lake District

6 Return a few yards along the path and go up the steps, now on the left, and follow the path to a second, upper bridge with a different view of the falls. Over the top bridge, bear right to walk with the river on your right to **High Force** and another bridge.

7 Cross this bridge and bear left to continue by the river, now on the right-hand bank and through a gate onto the open fell. You soon reach the gate in the wall that you passed through soon after the start of the walk. From here retrace your steps back to **Dockray**. (If you started at Aira Force and do not wish to go to the pub, turn right on a signed permissive path just before the second gate – point 2.)

Place of interest nearby

Ullswater is the second largest lake and is 7 miles long. The geology of the surrounding area is very varied and it was formed by three glaciers, which account for its serpentine shape and the variety of scenery surrounding it. Having admired the lake from above, enjoy it from a different angle by taking a trip on one of the steamers that ply the water. The full trip round the lake takes well over two hours but if time is more limited, you can just enjoy the short excursion from Glenridding or Pooley Bridge to Howtown. For details of the timetable ☎ 017684 82229 or visit www.ullswater-steamers.co.uk.

Langstrath Country Inn

This is a magnificent walk in Borrowdale, a valley that many, including Wainwright, consider to be the very best in this area of outstanding scenery: a lush valley surrounded by towering fells, woods ablaze with colour in autumn, a crystal clear river with its deep and mysterious pools and charming hamlets scattered around. No wonder it is so popular. Without great care

The Lake District

Distance – 6 miles.

OS Explorer OL4, The English Lakes North-western area. GR NY 263166.

Starting point Langstrath Country Inn, Stonethwaite.

How to get there *Follow the road through Borrowdale, the B5289. Take a minor road east which is signed 'Church ¼ Stonethwaite ½' and also for the Langstrath Country Inn where this walk starts.*

Alternatives *Parking at the pub is very limited but there is some roadside parking on the lane leading to Stonethwaite. In that case, continue along the lane into the village to the phone box referred to in 1 below and turn left. Alternatively, there are two possible car parks. One at Rosthwaite (charge) is signed from the main road and passed in point 3. The other is at Seatoller (National Trust, charge for non-members): take the path from the rear of the car park to pick up the route at point 10. There are a couple of hotels in Rosthwaite with public bars and also a teashop.*

and skilful management it could easily be loved to death so it is fortunate that it is mostly in the care of the National Trust. The route includes a pleasant stroll along the bank of the River Derwent, where there are many delightful spots to linger and to even take a dip on a hot day (they do happen occasionally in the Lakes!). This is by no means a difficult walk but there is a very short tricky stretch of about 50 yards by the river where you have to pick your way over some rocks.

THE PUB

Originally a 16th-century miner's cottage, **Langstrath Country Inn** has been developed into a charming hotel, with a welcoming public bar that has an open fire. There are also some tables outside for fine days. The possibilities for lunch range from filled baguettes to local potted shrimps or a cheese platter served with their own pickled onions and damson cheese to a Cumbrian gammon steak with eggs and chips. They always have four real ales on tap.

Lunches are served between noon and 2.30 pm every day except Monday ☎ 017687 77239; www.thelangstrath.com.

1 From the pub turn right back along the lane to a telephone box. Turn right along a track signed 'Greenup Edge Grasmere' and follow this over a bridge across a river to a T-junction.

2 Turn left, signed 'Watendlath via Rosthwaite', and walk along this to a surfaced cross track.

3 Turn left, re-crossing the river, to a road. Turn left for 40 yards then turn right on a tiny lane. When this bends sharp left at **Yew Tree Farm** (teashop) continue in the same direction over cobbles and between buildings, signed 'Footpath to Grange' and press on to the river and then beside it as far as a bridge.

4 Over the bridge turn right and continue along the riverbank ignoring all paths to the left. At one point the 'main' path veers left away from the river for a while but there is a right of way along the riverbank (not recommended after wet weather) and the main path is shortly rejoined.

5 Soon after this the path bears left up and away from the river to some large cairns. After passing through a gap in the wall go ahead on the path up to a T-junction. Turn right and follow the path down towards the river again.

The Lake District

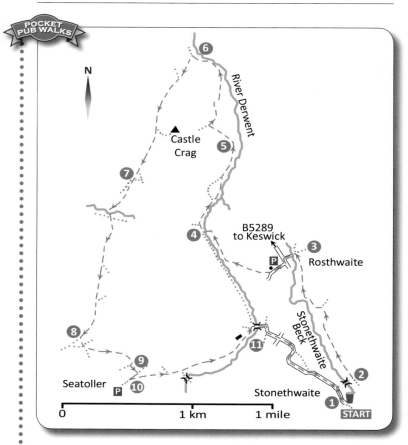

6 Just before reaching a footbridge turn left, back uphill, signed 'Seatoller 2 miles Honister 3 miles'. This path climbs steadily.

7 Just over the brow of the hill by a long cairn, take the centre one of three paths, signed 'Seatoller' Follow this path as it contours

round the hillside with magnificent views of Upper Borrowdale in every direction.

3 Eventually the path comes to two small gates within a small walled area. Go through the left-hand gate and follow what is soon a track, ignoring all paths to left and right and passing through a gate across the track. Continue down to a second gate. Through this gate continue on for another 60 yards to just after a right-hand bend.

9 Turn left down a very steep, grassy path. Do not cross a stream but turn right beside it for a few yards to a cross path. Turn right for just over 100 yards to find a path on the left in front of a stone wall. This is about 20 yards before a gate across the path, which leads to the car park at **Seatoller**.

0 Turn sharp left. Stay on this path as it contours round the hillside and then approaches the **River Derwent** again. There is now the tricky stretch referred to in the introduction but the path very soon improves.

1 Pass by **Borrowdale Youth Hostel**. Follow the drive over a bridge and continue, away from the river, along what is now a lane to a road. Take the lane opposite back to **Stonethwaite**.

Place of interest nearby

A visit to **Keswick brewery**, one of the many small breweries now found across the Lake District, is an enjoyable way to see how the beers are made and sample more of them. Booking is essential for tours, and dates and times can be found on their website, www.keswickbrewery.co.uk, or ☎ 017687 80700.

The Swan Hotel

This walk, at the heart of central Lakeland, captures everything that makes the Lake District so special. It combines fells, woodland, river and lakeside paths, with superb views and an interesting and historic village. Wordsworth lived in or near Grasmere for most of his adult life, an area so beautiful he described it as 'The most loveliest spot that man hath found'. Grasmere is therefore a place of literary pilgrimage but even without these associations it would be a honey-pot for tourists due to its central position and lovely setting. So, on parts of this walk you will probably meet other walkers but other sections are less well trod and more peaceful.

Distance – 5 miles.

OS Explorer OL7 The English Lakes South-eastern area. GR NY 339082.

Starting point The Swan Hotel.

How to get there *The Swan is just north of the village of Grasmere on the A591, Ambleside–Keswick road.*

Alternative *If you wish to visit the pub part way round the walk, start at White Moss car park (charge), NY 348065, on the A591 south of Grasmere. This is in two parts, one each side of the road. The route passes the section to the east of the road. This is the second section reached travelling north from Ambleside, on the right. You would then start the walk at point 5.*

THE PUB The **Swan** dates from the middle of the 17th century when it was built as a coaching inn on the main road between Ambleside and Keswick, now the A591. It was well known to Wordsworth and his visitors. Wordsworth refers to the pub in his poem *The Waggoner*, and asks 'Who does not know the famous Swan?' a line which is quoted on the Swan's sign to this day. Today it is quite a posh hotel but retains a welcoming walkers' bar. There are some interesting dishes on the menu, including haggis and neaps, with whiskey and mustard sauce on my visit. There is also a pleasant, lawned garden, with views of Helm Crag.

Food is available all day. ☎ *01539 435624; www.macdonaldhotels. co.uk/swan.*

The Lake District

1. Follow the lane next to the **Swan** between the building and main car park. Take the first lane on the right and follow it for about 300 yards, as far as a sharp right-hand bend.

2. On the bend turn left through a gate on a permitted path. Go past a building on the left to find a path behind the building that starts between walls to very shortly reach a gate. Through the gate, follow the path round to the right then along the hillside, first climbing gently for some great views of **Grasmere**, both lake and village. The path then descends, crossing a pretty waterfall, before a short climb leads to a T-junction with a larger public footpath.

3. Turn right, downhill, to a lane.

4. Turn left, signed 'Coffin route to Rydal'. At the far end of **White Moss** tarn on the left, bear right downhill, ignoring an immediate path leading right, to reach the main road adjacent to White Moss car park.

5. Cross the road and take a signed footpath to soon reach a roughly-surfaced path. Turn right along this, passing a picnic area by the river, to a bridge over the water. Cross the bridge and immediately turn right beside the river to the lake. Continue ahead on the path round the lake, ignoring all paths to the left.

The River Rothay

6. Eventually this wonderful path is forced left away from the lake up to a lane.

7. Turn right along the lane to **Grasmere** village. Carry on

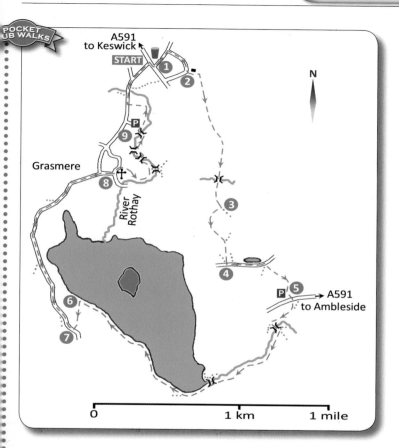

along the lane, signed 'Ambleside', to a T-junction, opposite the church.

3 Turn left past the churchyard, gingerbread shop and daffodil garden then turn right on a surfaced path signed 'Riverside Path'.

The Lake District

This leads to and then beside the river. Cross the river when there is no alternative (the second bridge). Do not cross back at the next bridge, which is private, but continue to the bridge after that. Now cross back into a car park. Turn right through the car park to walk with the river on the right. At the end of the car park, carry on along the riverside path and stay on the path as it bears left away from the river to a road.

9 Turn right along the road to the 'A' road and the **Swan**.

Places of interest nearby

Born in Cockermouth in 1770, William Wordsworth and his sister Dorothy lived in **Dove Cottage** on the outskirts of Grasmere from 1799 until 1808 and it was his home when he wrote what many consider his finest work. It is open to the public from 9.30 am every day except over Christmas and early January to early February, with last admission at 5 pm in summer and 4 pm in winter. ☎ 015394 35544; www.wordsworth.org.uk. The poet is buried in the churchyard of St Oswald's alongside his wife, their family and his sister.

Grasmere is not all about literature. The village is also home to the **Heaton Cooper Studio**, where there is a permanent display of work of the artists Alfred and William Heaton Cooper, father and son, both of whom are recognized as foremost watercolour artists of the area. The building occupied by the Gingerbread Shop was built in 1687 and used as the village schoolroom. Wordsworth taught there for a while. In 1854 it was let to Sarah Nelson who started making the hard and spicy gingerbread sold to this day. The recipe is a closely-guarded secret, kept locked in a bank vault.

7 Jenkin Crag & Waterhead

The Wateredge Inn

Starting almost at the head of Windermere, this walk begins with a gentle stroll by the lake, passing the site of a Roman fort and through a nature reserve, with a wonderful display of wild flowers in season. This should get the blood flowing for a short but energetic climb to a spectacular viewpoint before the route returns to Waterhead, passing Stagshaw Gardens.

The Lake District

Distance – 3 miles.

OS Explorer OL7, The English Lakes South-eastern area. GR NY 375033.

Starting point The Wateredge Inn, Waterhead. The pub car park is usually very busy so it is better to use the village car park (charge), across the road from the inn.

How to get there Waterhead is on the A5075, just after it branches off the A591, Windermere–Ambleside road.

Alternatives If you wish to visit the pub part way round this walk, after the climb to Jenkin Crag, start at Low Fold car park (charge). This is on the A591 about half way between Ambleside and Waterhead, almost opposite a large garden centre. Grid reference: NY377077. An unusual alternative refreshment stop is the youth hostel at Waterhead, housed in old hotel buildings with another superb view across the lake. Youth hostels have changed a lot since my young days and this one has a café (noon to 8 pm), with a bar serving a good choice of local ales. It is open between noon and 8 pm. The youth hostel is passed during point 11.

THE PUB The outstanding feature of the **Wateredge Inn** at Waterhead is its position on the shore at the head of the lake. The gardens lead down to the water and there are spectacular views across Windermere. Floor to ceiling windows mean the views can be enjoyed just as much in less than clement weather. The lunch menu caters to all tastes ranging from a choice of sandwiches through substantial platters, such as the hikers' one of ham and cheese, to full meals. There is a selection of real ales on offer including Theakston's bitter, Red Barn ale and Academy at the time of writing.

Lunch is served between noon and 2.30 pm, with light snacks available all day. ☎ *015394 32332; web site: www.wateredgeinn.co.uk.*

1 Turn left out of the **Wateredge Inn** or right out of the public car park, which is on the opposite side of the road. After a few yards turn left into a park and head to the lake. Turn right to walk beside the lake. At the far end of the park, when the path

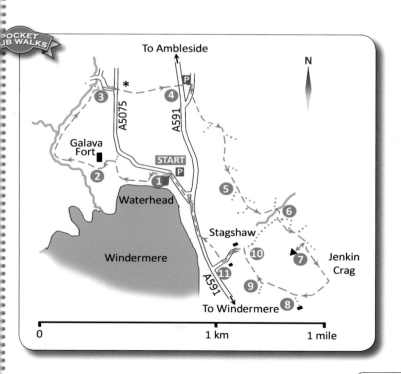

turns right back to the road, go through a metal kissing gate in the wall to **Borran's Field** containing the remains of the Roman fort.

2 Bear half left across the field, inspecting the remains, with their information plaques as you go, to a gate into **Birdhouse Meadow**. Follow the path as it bends right beside the river, past the confluence of the **River Brathay** and the **River Rothay**, to eventually reach a road.

(Note: the path across Birdhouse Meadow may be flooded in winter. Also, the path by the river is not a public footpath and access is at the discretion of the landowner. It is a popular path but could be withdrawn. If the path is impassable for either reason, go through the gate from Borrans Field onto the road and turn left to pick up the route again at * below.)

3 Turn right along the road to shortly reach a road junction. Cross the road (*) and maintain direction along a fenced path that emerges on a main road opposite **Low Fold** car park.

4 Cross the road and car park to a lane at the rear and turn right. Take the first left, signed 'Jenkins Crag, Skelghyll and Troutbeck'. Follow the surfaced track up and when it forks take the right branch, signed 'Jenkyns Crag'. The track contours along the hillside with superb views on the right over the head of **Windermere** and up the **Langdale Valley**. At the next fork, again take the right option to continue along the hillside.

5 On entering **Skelghyll Woods** ignore a path on the right to continue uphill on the main path. Pass the private entrance to Skelghyll Woods and then fork left on a path signed 'Jenkyns Crag and Troutbeck'.

6 Follow the main path round to the right to cross the beck. Ignore all paths on the right and left and continue up to **Jenkyns Crag**.

Jenkin Crag & Waterhead

Turn right through a gap in the wall at the Jenkyn's Crag sign to the viewpoint.

7 From the viewpoint return towards the main path. Do **not** go through the gap in the wall onto the main path. Instead, just before the wall, take a smaller path on the right downhill. This soon curves right and goes steeply downhill through a wooded area.

8 Turn right on a crossing path leading from a house.

9 When the main path turns very sharply left, maintain direction on a smaller path. Follow this to join a track.

10 Turn left to pass **Stagshaw Gardens** on the right after 40 yards.

11 Just after a stone barn on the left, turn right on a path between a wall and a fence and follow this to the road. Turn right. There is a footway on the opposite side of this busy road. At the traffic lights bear left back to the **Wateredge Inn**.

Place of interest nearby

Stagshaw Gardens, passed towards the end of this walk, were created by the late C. H. D. Acland, a keen gardener, who was regional agent for the National Trust for nearly 30 years. An area of scrubby woodland was transformed into a series of glades, with rhododendrons, azaleas and a wide variety of other shrubs thriving under the thinned oaks. It is essentially a spring garden and is open every day from April until the end of June from 10 am to 6.30 pm. ☎ 015394 46027.

The Britannia

This outstanding walk at the heart of the Lake District cannot be recommended too highly. Indeed, if someone could only do one walk and wanted a taste of everything the Lakes has to offer, this is the one I would recommend. It has unforgettable views throughout, rising to a memorable climax

Distance – 4½ miles.

OS Explorer OL7, The English Lakes South-eastern area. GR NY 328048.

Starting point The Britannia Inn, Elterwater. The Britannia has virtually no parking of its own. There is a National Trust car park (charge) across the road. There is no street parking in Elterwater and few spots on the road into the village. Alternatively, there is a public car park for Elterwater just off the B5343 from where you can walk into the village to start the walk.

How to get there From Ambleside take the A593 Coniston road. At Skelwith Bridge bear right on the B5343 Langdales road. Turn left into Elterwater village. The car park is just before the river on the left.

Alternatives The route passes the Skelwith Bridge Hotel, which has a public bar, the Talbot, at point 2.

from Little Loughrigg – much better than Loughrigg, its more lofty neighbour, in my opinion. The route also visits a waterfall, a lake and a beautifully situated tarn.

THE PUB The **Britannia** is perhaps the most famous and popular pub in this part of the Lake District. A whitewashed freehouse, it stands at the centre of Elterwater village amidst the dramatic scenery of the Langdale valley. It was built over 400 years ago as a gentleman farmer's house, and within its thick stone walls is a warren of small and cosy rooms, with low-beamed oak ceilings and coal fires in winter. There is extensive seating outside at the front as well, necessary because there is no way all the customers

The Lake District

could fit inside on a busy day. The food is unpretentious, tasty and served in generous portions. The full menu changes from day to day but nearly always features the delicious lamb Henry; it is very sustaining so perhaps is best enjoyed at the end of a walk! Resident beers include Coniston Brewery's Bluebird, Thwaites' Wainwright, Langdale Tup and their own recipe 'Britannia Special' which Coniston Brewery produce exclusively for the Britannia. In addition, they have two pumps for guest beers, which change regularly.

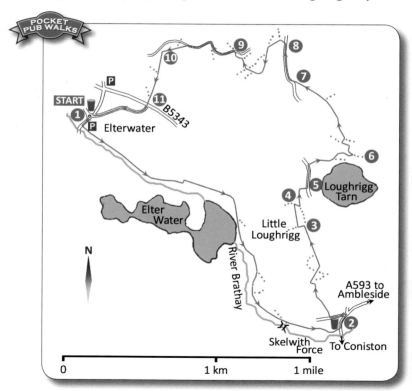

Elterwater & Little Loughrigg

The Britannia is open all day every day, with the lunchtime menu available between noon and 2 pm but snacks, including scones and cream, are served in the afternoon as well. ☎ *015394 37210; www.britinn.net.*

1 Turn right out of the **Britannia** along the road. Immediately before a bridge over the river turn left on a riverside path and follow this, pausing to enjoy the magnificent view across **Elterwater** to the **Langdales** beyond. Continue on the main path, passing **Skelwith Force**, and continue through the slateworks and past **Chesters** café and shop (worth a visit) to a road.

2 Turn left then first left. Opposite the **Talbot** turn right through a gate on a signed path. Follow this up the field to a gate then on between a wall and a fence to a gate into **Neaum Crag**, an estate of log cabins. Keep ahead along the surfaced drive, ignoring all side turns and cross drives and following the yellow arrow waymarks. The drive climbs steeply. When it ends, continue on the path ahead to a gate onto the fell side.

3 Through the gate turn left, up by a wall, for about 30 yards. At the highest point turn right on a path that soon leads up to a crag. After admiring the views of both the **Langdales** and **Loughrigg** tarn, continue along the path to a T-junction with a cross path.

4 Turn right to a second T-junction. Now turn left and follow the path to a lane.

5 Turn left for about 150 yards then turn right on a signed path that leads past the end of **Loughrigg** tarn, crossing a ladder stile. When the path forks a few yards after the stile, bear left up to a gate onto a track.

6 Turn left along the track for about 200 yards. Note a bench on the right. Some 40 yards after the bench, turn right on a path that

The Lake District

shortly reaches a gate. Through the gate, turn left, signed 'Loughrigg Fell', and follow the path beside the fence and then a wall. Ignore a stepped path on the right (unless you fancy nipping up Loughrigg Fell) and continue on the path contouring round the hillside to a lane.

7 Turn right for about 250 yards.

8 Bear left through a small gate next to a field gate. After 30 yards bear left to stay on the main path. Ignore all paths to left and right and follow this to a lane.

9 Turn left for about 350 yards. Bear left on a track that cuts across a bend in the road; this is the old road.

10 At the point where the track rejoins the road turn left on a clear path and follow this down to a road.

11 Turn left for a few yards then turn right and follow the road into **Elterwater** village and the **Britannia** ahead.

Place of interest nearby

Just over the hill from Elterwater lies **Grasmere** where Wordsworth lived for most of his adult life (see walk 6). From 1813 until his death in 1850 at the age of 80, Wordsworth lived at **Rydal Mount** between Grasmere and Ambleside, where he enjoyed life as the lynch pin of the Lakeland intelligentsia and a national institution. It was here that he wrote many of his poems, revised and improved much of his earlier works and published the final version of his most famous poem *Daffodils*. Rydal Mount is open to the public for much of the year and visitors can wander through the house and extensive gardens landscaped by the poet. ☎ 015394 33002; www.rydalmount.co.uk.

9 **Nether Wasdale & Wastwater**

The Strands Inn

Wastwater **is one of the** more remote lakes in the National Park and is very distinctive. Towering over the southern shore are the Wasdale screes, a steep fell-side crumbling into the dark water beneath. The sheet of water leads to a backdrop of some of the most majestic fells such as Scafell and Great Gable. The prospect from the end of the lake was voted

The Lake District

Distance – 5 miles.

OS Explorer OL6 The English Lakes South-western area. GR SD 124040.

Starting point The Strands Inn, Nether Wasdale.

How to get there From the A595, Barrow to Whitehaven road, at Gosforth take a minor road east to Wasdale. After three miles bear right to Nether Wasdale. It may also be reached from the central Lakes via Hardknott and Wrynose passes to Eskdale then on to Santon Bridge and follow the Gosforth road to Nether Wasdale.

Alternative The only alternative starting point is roadside parking just before the bridge at the end of point 1.

'Britain's Favourite View' in the TV programme of the same name in 2005. Comparatively few people enjoy it because you have to walk there – and that is where this route goes. Choose a clear and sunny day (Wastwater is definitely not at its scenic best in Lakeland drizzle), preferably with a dusting of snow on the tops and I guarantee you will not be disappointed – and don't forget your camera!

THE PUB The **Strands Inn** in Nether Wasdale was built around 1800 as a hotel and post house. Since 2007 they have had their own micro-brewery brewing just for the Strands so you will be able to enjoy beers you cannot taste elsewhere. Snacks are not available on Sunday but you can always enjoy something from the starter menu for a light lunch. As well as the traditional, beamed interior, there is a pleasant garden for warmer days.

Bar meals are served throughout the year from 12 noon till 2.30 pm and the evening menu is available from 5.30 pm till 9 pm Monday to Saturday. On Sunday food is served from 12 noon till 8 pm. ☎ 01946 726237; www.thestrandsinn.com.

1. Turn right out of the **Strands Inn** and walk along the road out of the village to a road junction. Bear right, signed 'Santon Bridge 2 Drigg 6' and follow the road over a bridge, ignoring a lane on the left.

2. Some 30 yards after crossing the bridge, turn left along the track to Easthwaite Farm, signed 'Wasdale'. Press on through the farmyard to continue along the track, ignoring a path on the right.

3. As the track bends right, turn left off the track on a waymarked path to walk along the left-hand side of a field to a river. Turn left on a riverside path for a few yards to a bridge over the river.

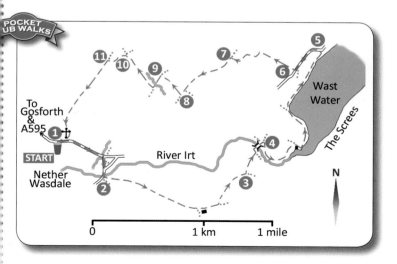

4 Over the bridge, do not follow the obvious riverside path to the left but go through a kissing gate ahead to a fork after a few yards. Bear right and follow the path through the woods, ignoring a path on the left, to reach a boathouse and the end of the lake. Carry on beside the lake, soon reaching the classic viewpoint up the lake with the screes looming over it and the panorama of fells beyond the head of the valley. There is a seat well placed to admire it. Eventually the lakeside path reaches a ladder stile then climbs up to a lane.

There is said to be a gnome garden complete with picket fence at the bottom of Wastwater. It was apparently removed by police divers at the behest of the National Park Authority after some divers died after spending too long too deep searching for the little fellows. However, the rumour is that it has been replaced at a greater depth, beyond that to which the police are allowed to dive by their elf and safety rules!

5 Turn left along the lane for about 350 yards.

6 Turn right on a signed path along a track to a gate. The walled enclosure on the right was the kitchen garden of **Wasdale Hall**. Through the gate, carry on along the path as it bears left and wends its way across a possibly boggy moss to a T-junction with a cross path marked by a finger post, broken at the time of writing.

7 Turn left and follow the path through a gate and past a rocky outcrop.

8 Shortly after the path is enclosed between wire fences and immediately after a second gate, turn right on a path signed 'Buckbarrow' and similarly enclosed to reach two gateways. Continue through the one on the right to a T-junction with a bridleway in front of a fence.

9 Turn left. Go across a bridge over a stream then walk across a field to a gate. Immediately through the gate turn right to walk with a wall on the right as far as a finger post, rather broken at the time of writing, marking a cross path.

10 Turn left (the easiest place is just before the post). The path is not visible on the ground at the time of writing but goes over the low hill somewhat to the right of its highest point to a broken-down wall. Cross the wall and walk up a field to a cross path on the far side in front of a wall.

11 Turn left to shortly go through a dogleg in the wall. When the wall then veers away to the left, keep ahead to a boardwalk and stile over a wall. Now follow the path down through gorse and ahead through a campsite, passing to the right of a play area and to the left of the toilet block. Continue along the drive to the road in **Nether Wasdale** and turn right back to the pub.

Places of interest nearby

For further magnificent views of **Wasdale**, drive along the minor road from Nether Wasdale beside the lake, crossed at point 5 on the walk, to **Wasdale Head**. Wasdale is a place that invites superlatives: not only England's highest mountain (Scafell) and deepest lake but also England's smallest church (though this is disputed) and once home to England's biggest liar. This was 19th-century publican Will Ritson, who loved to regale his customers with whoppers. For example, he claimed that Wasdale turnips are so big they could be used as sheds once Sunday lunch had been quarried out of them. An annual greatest liar competition is held at the Bridge Inn in Santon Bridge in his honour.

10 Eskdale & Muncaster Fell

The King George IV Inn

This walk, in the far western reaches of the Lake District, explores a long tongue of fell that separates the valleys of the rivers Esk and Mite before they flow into the sea at Ravenglass. For all its modest height at 231 metres, there are splendid views of the Lake District mountains and the Cumbrian coast from Muncaster Fell. There is far more to this expedition than an invigorating walk over a minor fell, though. Just getting to the start can be an adventure as the obvious route from the

Distance – 5 miles.

OS Explorer OL6 The English Lakes South-western area. GR SD 148998.

Starting point: King George IV, Eskdale Green. The pub does not have a large car park but some road parking is possible nearby.

How to get there From the central Lake District, Eskdale can be reached via Wrynose and Hard Knot passes. Alternatively, from A595, the Cumbrian coast road, about 2 miles north of Ravenglass, take a minor road signed 'Irton, Santon Bridge and Eskdale Green'.

Alternatives If you wish to visit the pub part way round this walk, start at Muncaster Mill station SD 095976. This is accessed from the A595 just north of Ravenglass and there is a small car park for people using the railway. You would then start the walk at point 10. There is also a car park at Eskdale Green station SD 145998 (point 2). There is no other source of refreshment on this walk.

central Lake District is via Hard Knott and Wrynose passes to Eskdale. This is recognised as the most challenging road in the Lake District, narrow with many hairpin bends and a 1 in 3 gradient in places. Go via the coast road, the A595, if you are worried by this. The walk itself is varied and interesting, with both woodland and fell walking and a visit to a pretty tarn.

Finally, the return to the start is by an entertaining ride on a unique narrow-gauge railway, the 'Ratty', which runs up Eskdale from Ravenglass. This route is only feasible when this is in operation so it is important to check the timetable and plan

The Lake District

your day accordingly. (01229 717171 or www.ravenglass-railway.co.uk). The train arrives at Muncaster Mill station, where we catch the train, about five minutes after it leaves Ravenglass.

THE PUB

It is said that there has been an inn on this site since the Romans passed by on their way to Ravenglass. The **King George IV Inn**, Eskdale Green, has a cosy and welcoming atmosphere with open fires, oak beamed ceilings and original slate flagged floors so walkers and their dogs are welcome. Food covers the full spectrum from light snacks to hearty fare and includes daily specials such as, on my visit, mutton and black pudding pie. There are also some very tempting puddings. The King George offers a good choice of well-kept local real ales.

Food is available all day. ☎ 01946 723470; www.kinggeorge-eskdale.co.uk.

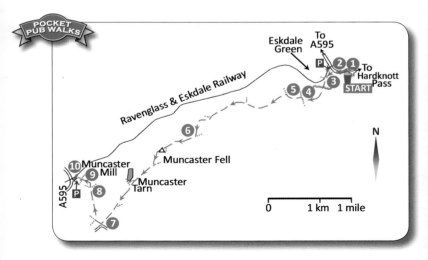

1 Turn left out of the pub and walk along the road to **Eskdale Green** station.

2 Take a track on the left, signed 'Muncaster Head ½ mile, Muncaster Fell 1½ miles', and ignore an immediate track on the right to the station and its car park.

3 Just before the track crosses the railway line, bear left on a waymarked bridleway. Follow the path through a gate and over a stream. On reaching an open area, keep to the right by a stone wall. When the wall turns right, leave the wall and continue in much the same direction across an open area towards **Muncaster Fell**, seen ahead, to a track.

4 Turn right, through a field gate, and walk along the track for 25 yards then turn left uphill on a path. Follow this up to a gate. Go through the gate and continue for about 70 yards.

5 Turn left on a clear path. Follow this up the fell side then down into a dip. Ignore a path to the right at the bottom of the dip and continue upwards, eventually walking with a wall on the right. The path forks about 25 yards after the wall ends; take either branch as they rejoin a little further on. Press on as the path wends its way through boggy areas to finally arrive at a T-junction with a cross path.

The 'Ratty' narrow gauge railway

6 Turn right. Follow the path as it meanders across the fell. Ignore a path leading left before a final steep climb leads to a trig point – a good

The Lake District

place for a rest with magnificent 360° views encompassing both the mountains of the Lake District and the Cumbrian coast. From the trig point continue in the same direction and press on as the path becomes more of a track. It soon passes close to **Muncaster tarn** on the right. For a better look at this jewel-like miniature lake, surrounded by trees and studded with water lilies, bear right on a path that rejoins the main track a little further on. Eventually the track reaches a main road.

7 Turn immediately right on a track signed 'Muncaster Mill via Branken Wall'. At a track on the left turn right through a gate and follow the woodland path for about ½ mile to a three-way fork.

8 Take the centre one of three paths and follow this down to a track.

9 Turn left along the track, ignoring an immediate path on the left signed 'Ravenglass', to a drive. Turn right to **Muncaster Mill** station.

10 Catch the train to **Eskdale Green** station. From the station walk to the road and turn right to the **King George IV**.

Places of interest nearby

This walk follows Roman footsteps, where the mountains sweep down to the coast. **Ravenglass** is an ancient port. Called Glannaventa in Roman times, it was garrisoned by a fort that accommodated up to 1,000 men. **Walls Castle**, well signed from the A595, is the remains of the bath house. It is the only part of the fort still visible and the walls still stand 12 feet high, the tallest Roman remains in the north of England. Walls Castle was identified as the bath house in 1928 and an explanatory plaque on the site tells you more. Walls Castle is cared for by English Heritage and is freely accessible.

11 Staveley

The Eagle & Child

This is a varied walk in the attractive, undulating southern part of the National Park. The route climbs steadily from the ancient community of Staveley to Potter Fell and then descends via two tarns to join the Dales Way beside the River Kent back to the village. This charming section is an interesting contrast to the woods and fells explored in the first part of the route and this stretch of the river is rich in wildlife, especially birds.

The Lake District

Distance – 5½ miles.

OS Explorer OL7 The English Lakes South-eastern area.

Starting point The Eagle & Child, Staveley. GR SD 472980.

How to get there From the A591 leading south from the Lake District towards Kendal, take a road on the left signed 'Staveley Kentmere' to the Eagle & Child on the right at the far end of the village. Travelling north along the A591, take the road to Staveley to find the pub on the left soon after you enter the village.

Alternatives The car park at the Eagle & Child is not large. The best alternative is to use Mill Yard car park (SD 471982) signed from Main Street, Staveley. Take the path signed 'Riverside Walk' from the car park to a bridge over the river to pick up the route at point 2. The only other sources of refreshment on this walk are the other establishments in Staveley, including the estimable Wilf's café in Mill Yard.

THE PUB When pubs were proper pubs, the award-winning **Eagle & Child** is what proper pubs used to be like and occasionally still are – a friendly and cosy establishment that has met travellers' needs since the 18th century, including that indefatigable pair, Dorothy and William Wordsworth. It is pleasant at all times of year, with an open fire in winter and a super garden overlooking the confluence of the rivers Kent and Gowan for warmer days. As a freehouse, they offer a wide range of real ales with five hand-pulled beers on at any one time and these often include beers from Hawkshead Brewery based in the village. The food caters for all appetites from snacks to full meals.

Food is available every day except Christmas Day between noon and 2.30 pm and in the evening. ☎ 01539 821320; website: www. eaglechildinn.co.uk.

1 Turn left out of the **Eagle and Child** into **Staveley** as far as **Margaret's Tower** on the right. Immediately after the tower turn right on a footpath signed 'Riverside Walk' and follow this to a bridge over a river.

2 Over the bridge turn right to walk between a wall and the river. When the wall ends, turn left to continue with a wall on the left to a track. Cross the track and continue through a gate next to a field gate and walk up to a lane.

3 Turn right. When the lane forks after about 100 yards, bear left and follow the lane round a left-hand bend as far as a sharp right-hand bend.

4 Leave the lane on the right-hand bend and go ahead into the aptly-named **Craggy Wood**. Turn right and follow the main path as it zig-zags up through the wood and then left along the top of the crags. Pass through a gap in a wall and press on along the path to eventually reach a stone stile in a wall.

5 Over the stile turn right through a gateway or over an adjacent stile. The path is not always visible on the ground but is easy to navigate from stile to stile. It eventually descends between farm buildings to a lane.

6 Turn right for about 400 yards.

7 Turn left on a track to **Birk Field**. Follow a path through a field gate to the right of a garage, passing the farmhouse. In front of a gate and wall, turn right to walk with a stream on your right to a gate. Go ahead through a second gate and up to a third.

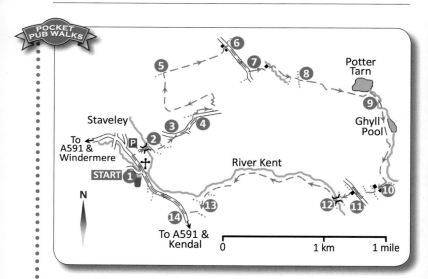

8 Turn right for 20 yards then left on a faint path, signed 'Potter Tarn'. Follow this up to a gap in a wall and on to a gate on the left. Through the gate, continue uphill, heading slightly right on an even fainter path that skirts to the left of a rounded hilltop to **Potter Tarn** on the left.

9 At the end of the tarn cross a ladder stile and go ahead to meet the exit stream. Turn right along the bank, crossing the stream twice, to a gate and on to pass **Ghyll Pool** on your left. Continue down to a gate and ahead downhill. Do not go through a gap in a wall ahead but turn left to pick up a track to the right of a stream and follow this downhill.

10 Turn right through a gate onto a walled track signed 'Hundhowe'. Pass a farm and continue on the main track to a lane.

1 Turn right for about 200 yards. Just after **Hagg Foot Farm**, turn left on a signed footpath along a concrete farm drive. Follow this past farm buildings then turn right on an unsurfaced track down to a bridge over the **River Kent**.

2 Immediately over the bridge turn right along a riverside path and follow it up river for about a mile. The path eventually becomes a track.

3 After going through a gate, bear left off the track across a small field to a gate. Through the gate, turn right on a signed path and follow a wall to a gate onto a walled path. Turn right to a road.

4 Turn right along the footway and follow this back to the start.

Place of interest nearby

Hawkshead Brewery, in Mill Yard, Staveley, is one of a number of small breweries scattered across the Lakes whose products are available in many of the pubs featured in this book. It started life in a barn in Hawkshead in 2002 but quickly needed larger premises to keep up with demand and moved to a purpose-built brewery in Staveley in 2006. Brewery tours are available on Saturdays at 2 pm and the Beer Hall is open every day from noon. ☎ 01539 825260; www.hawksheadbrewery.co.uk.

12 Coniston & Tarn Hows

The Crown Inn

This superb walk visits some of the loveliest landscape in the Lake District. Created by Nature, skilfully augmented by the Victorian owners, made accessible to us all by the generosity of Beatrix Potter and now lovingly managed by the National Trust, the Monk Coniston estate is outstanding and much of it is explored on this walk. Starting in Coniston, the route climbs to Tarn Hows, often described as the prettiest spot in the Lake District. The path then leads to Monk Coniston, visiting the newly-restored walled garden (no charge) before returning to

Distance – 5 miles.

OS Explorer OL7 The English Lakes South-eastern area. GR NY 303976.

Starting point The Crown Inn, Tilberthwaite Avenue, Coniston. The main public car park for Coniston (charge) is across the road from the Crown.

How to get there Coniston is on the A593. The Crown is on the B5285, the Hawkshead road, in the village.

Alternatives There are other pubs in Coniston, notably the Black Bull and Sun, but not so well placed for this route. Parking is also available in Shepherds Bridge Lane (point 2) where at quiet times of year you may be able to park on the roadside and Coniston Sports Club allows parking in its car park at a somewhat lower rate than the public car park. If you wish to visit Coniston part way round the walk, start at Tarn Hows where there is a National Trust car park (hefty charge for non-members). You would then start the walk at point 6.

Coniston Water and the bustling village that takes its name. This expedition is not long or arduous but do allow plenty of time to pause and enjoy the wonderful scenery all around.

THE PUB

The **Crown Inn** in Coniston is a traditional Robinson's house, with a welcoming wood-panelled bar and some tables outside. The food is substantial and tasty pub fare, including a selection of sandwiches and filled jacket potatoes for a lighter lunch through to pub favourites such as Cumberland sausage and mash with onion gravy or pie of the day.

The Lake District

Food is served every day from noon. Telephone: 015394 41243; www. crowninnconiston.com.

1 Turn left out of the **Crown** or right out of the car park. Turn left along **Shepherds Bridge Lane**.

2 Opposite **Coniston Primary School** turn right, over the river, on a signed path. Immediately across the bridge, turn left and follow

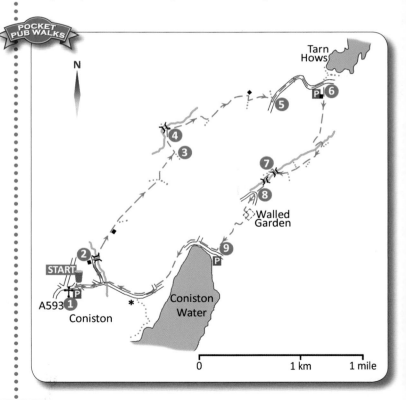

Coniston & Tarn Hows Walk 12

the path uphill, passing an unusual crenellated building, once the kennels for the fox hounds of the Monk Coniston estate and now an information point. Continue uphill, ignoring a path on the right, and into a wood then downhill. The path is now less obvious but keep ahead over the lawn-like grass. At the end of the wood on the right, bear left to a gate then go ahead again to a gate onto a track.

3 Turn left as far as a bridge over a beck.

4 Immediately before the bridge, turn right on a waymarked path across a field to a gate into woods. Follow the path up through the woods to a cottage. Turn right along the drive then follow it left to a lane.

5 Turn left along the lane as far as a car park on the right. Go a few yards beyond the car park for the best view of **Tarn Hows**.

The view from Monk Coniston walled garden

The Lake District

6 At the far end of the car park turn right on a path signed 'Coniston 2m'. Follow the main path gently downhill. Join a path coming in from the left, then bear right at a fork. Continue along the main path for about ¼ mile, ignoring paths to right and left.

7 Turn left down some steps on a permitted path signed 'Monk Coniston ¼' to cross a bridge and continue to a road.

8 Cross the road and go through a small wooden gate into the grounds of **Monk Coniston Hall** and follow the path into the walled garden. Leave the garden through a gate on the right and follow the path ahead, signed 'Lake'. Just after a seat on the right, go through a gate on the left and continue down towards the lake to a road.

9 Go through a gate and turn right on a path parallel with the road. Follow this back to **Coniston**.

Places of interest nearby

Brantwood, across the lake from Coniston village, was the home of John Ruskin, poet, artist and social reformer. The house and gardens are open to the public and there is an excellent restaurant with a terrace overlooking the lake. It is open throughout the year, closing on Monday and Tuesday in the winter. ☎ 015394 41396; www.brantwood.org.uk. You can reach Brantwood by car or by cruising across the lake on the National Trust's steam yacht *Gondola* (summer only, ☎ 015394 32733 or www.nationaltrust.org.uk/gondola)) or the solar powered launches that ply the lake. Timetables are widely available in the area; or ☎ 017687 75753; or online: www.conistonlaunch.co.uk. To reach the landing stage from the walk turn left on a track just after the Waterhead Hotel (* on map). There is limited parking near the landing stage.

The Tower Bank Arms

This is an easy and delightful walk exploring the countryside that Beatrix Potter loved. It visits the village of Near Sawrey where she bought her first Lakeland property, Hilltop, which is a Mecca for her many devotees today, especially Japanese visitors. The illustrations for the books did not spring

The Lake District

Distance – 4 miles.

OS Explorer OL7 The English Lakes South-eastern area. GR SD 371955.

Starting point: The walk as described below starts from the Tower Bank Arms in Near Sawrey. However, the popularity of Hilltop is such that parking here is **extremely** difficult at all but the quietest times of year. The Tower Bank Arms has almost no parking and the National Trust car park in the village is intended just for visitors to Hilltop. I do most strongly urge you to consider the alternative of starting at Far Sawrey.

How to get there The Sawreys are both on the B5285 between Hawkshead and the ferry to Bowness. Coming from Hawkshead, Near Sawrey is the first village you come to whereas coming from the ferry Far Sawrey is the first village.

Alternatives The village hall in Far Sawrey allows visitors to use their car park in return for a donation towards the upkeep of the building. (GR SD 379954). In that case, turn left out of the car park past the Sawrey Hotel to a surfaced track on the right (Cuckoo Brow Lane) to join the route at point 5. The hotel in Far Sawrey also has a public bar that serves food.

from her imagination but were drawn from life and the scenes can still be recognised today. These include the charming Moss Eccles tarn, visited en route, that appears in her book, *Jeremy Fisher*, and which she and her husband used to visit on summer evenings. It is a pleasing spot that may well tempt you to linger. There are great views across Esthwaite Water to Grizedale Forest beyond.

THE PUB

One building used by Beatrix Potter in *The Tale of Jemima Puddleduck* that can still be recognised today is the **Tower Bank Arms** in Near Sawrey, next door to Hilltop. The pub dates back to the 17th century and is now owned by the National Trust. There is an attractive garden to enjoy the views across the village. The lunch menu ranges from sandwiches to more substantial meals such as, at the time of writing, a steaming bowl of mussels. Local real ales on offer include Hawkshead Bitter and Bargates Catnap, as well as guest beers.

Food is served between noon and 2 pm every day and from 6 pm every day except Monday. Telephone: 015394 36334; www.towerbankarms.com.

1 Turn left out of **Tower Bank Arms** and walk through **Near Sawrey**, past the car park for **Hill Top**. Take a lane on the left signed 'Lakeside'. Ignore a lane on the right and turn left at the next junction, where there is a seat well placed to enjoy the superb view northwards towards the central fells. Walk along this quiet lane for about a further two-thirds of a mile, admiring the views across **Esthwaite Water** to **Grizedale**.

2 Take a public footpath on the left into woodland. Ignore paths on the right and left after a few yards and follow the waymarked path uphill through the woods to a gate into a field.

3 The path through the field is not very clear on the ground to begin with. It goes directly across a large field to a gate and then across a small field to another gate. In the third field bear left on a path beside a wire fence. Over a stile follow the path round to the right following a line of fine oaks to reach a lane.

4 Turn left into **Far Sawrey**. When the lane forks, bear left to a T-junction. (If you started in Far Sawrey, bear right here back to the village hall.)

The Lake District

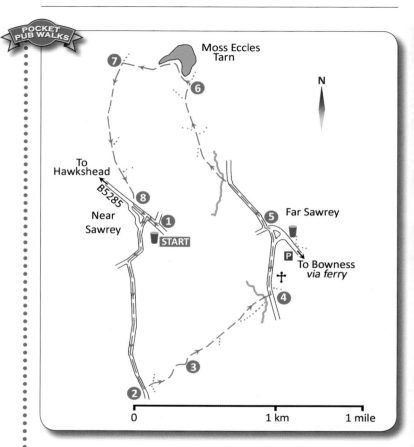

Moss Eccles
Tarn

7

6

N

To
Hawkshead

B5285

8

1

5 Far Sawrey

Near
Sawrey

START

P
To Bowness
via ferry

†

4

3

2

| 0 | 1 km | 1 mile |

5 At the T-junction turn left, then immediately right along a surfaced
drive, **Cuckoo Brow Lane**. About 100 yards after a gate and cattle
grid, bear left on an unsurfaced track, signed 'Claife Heights'.
Continue ahead, again signed 'Claife Heights' as a track joins on
the left.

6 Immediately after a gate across the main track, the wall on the left bears away from the track. Leave the track at this point and walk by the wall up a rise to **Moss Eccles tarn**. Take a permissive path to the left of the tarn to a gate. Through the gate, the path is not visible on the ground. Bear half right to eventually come to a track.

7 Turn left and follow the track downhill, with a wall on the right to a road.

8 Turn left and walk along the road into **Near Sawrey** and through the village to the **Tower Bank Arms**.

Place of interest nearby

Beatrix Potter, one of the National Trust's greatest benefactors, first came to Near Sawrey in 1896 when her parents took a house for a holiday. She fell in love with the area and was eventually able to buy **Hill Top**. She did not live there permanently and had a manager to look after the farm, but stayed for weeks on end. At this time she was at her most prolific and wrote thirteen books and every room contains a reference to a picture in a 'tale'. She bought more properties in the area with the profits and married the solicitor who had acted for her in the purchases. As Mrs William Heelis she was less interested in writing and more interested in farming. Hill Top is in the care of the National Trust and is open every day except Friday from mid February to October from 10.30 am. It is very small and a timed-ticket system is in operation to prevent overcrowding. ☎ 015394 36269.

14 **Grizedale Forest**

The Eagles Head

This is a gem of a walk through the quieter southern part of Grizedale Forest. It is essentially a woodland walk, mainly through areas of broadleaved oak and birch but with a seasoning of conifers too. The route also visits two excellent viewpoints and a series of pretty cascades, Force Falls, set in

Distance – 4½ miles.

OS Explorer OL7 The English Lakes South-eastern area. GR NY 338923.

Starting point The Eagles Head, Satterthwaite.

How to get there Satterthwaite is at the southern end of Grizedale. From the B5285 at the southern edge of Hawkshead, turn right to pass the school. After leaving the village, take the first road on the right, signed for Grizedale and Satterthwaite, and follow the road to Satterthwaite. The Eagles Head is on the right towards the far end of the village approaching from the north.

Alternatives The Eagles Head has very limited parking. It might be possible to find a parking spot elsewhere in the village at quiet times of year. A better alternative is to start the walk at Blind Lane car park, NY 343912. To get to this, follow the road south from Satterthwaite. When the road turns sharp right less than a mile south of the village, turn left to a small car park on the left after a couple of hundred yards. You will then start the walk at point 9. There is also a car park on the road about ¼ mile south of Satterthwaite. There is no other source of refreshment on this walk.

woodland carpeted with flowers in spring. Though this walk is not especially long or arduous, do allow plenty of time to enjoy the views. The route is rarely level for very long. The path down from Brock Crag is quite steep and rocky and needs sound footwear to walk in safety and comfort.

The Lake District

The **Eagles Head** in Satterthwaite is a traditional Lakeland pub housed in what was originally a farmhouse dating back to the 16th century. The building has been altered over the years but has still retained its old charm. A freehouse, the resident beers come from Moorhouse's brewery of Burnley and include Eagles Head Ale and Grized Ale, and there are regularly changing guest beers from local breweries. The Eagles Head is

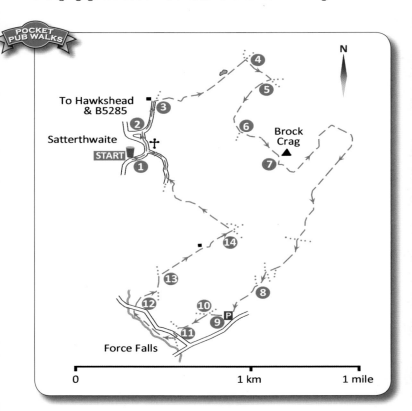

POCKET PUB WALKS

N

To Hawkshead & B5285

Satterthwaite

START

Brock Crag

Force Falls

| 0 | | 1 km | 1 mile |

particularly noted for its pies. Suggestions for lunch include soup and sandwiches, as well full meals and it is proud to serve local meat, which can be enjoyed as a sandwich filling.

Food is served every lunchtime and evening except Mondays (though food is available on Bank Holiday Mondays). Telephone: 01229 860237; www.eagleshead.co.uk.

1. Turn left out of the **Eagles Head** and walk through the village. Some 50 yards after the church, when the road bends left, keep ahead on a minor road to a T-junction with a lane.

2. Turn right and follow the lane uphill. Do turn round to admire the view as you climb **Breasty Haw**.

3. At a house called **Old Breasty Haw**, turn right on a bridleway, signed 'High Dale Park', soon passing a purple-topped waymark post, and climb to a cross track.

4. Turn right along the track to a T-junction.

5. Turn right, now with green waymark posts.

6. Take the first track on the left, waymarked with green and white topped posts. When the track ends, continue on the waymarked path, passing just below **Brock Crag**. It is well worth diverting a few yards onto the crag for the outstanding view.

7. Continue on the waymarked path as it wends its way down from the crag, then keep on the path as it circles the lower slopes and eventually becomes a forest track. Continue past a track on the left as far as a sharp right-hand bend in the track.

8. Turn left off the track on a path waymarked with the familiar green and white-topped posts. This leads through the end of a small car park, which is the alternative start.

9. Continue on the waymarked path from the rear left of the car park and follow it up to a T-junction.

The Lake District

10 Turn left. Follow the main path, ignoring all side paths to a lane.

11 Cross the lane a few yards to the left to carry on along the waymarked path, now leading right beside the beck and falls. The path eventually returns to the lane.

(The best views of the falls are gained by going further left before continuing the route. The lower falls can be accessed from the lane via a small gate just before a house.)

12 Cross the lane and walk along the track towards **Bowkerstead Farm** and **Grizedale campsite**, now with white-topped waymarks. Ignore a track on the right on a bend and carry on for about another 150 yards to a waymarked path on the right, signed 'Bowkerstead walk'.

13 Turn right and follow the path uphill to a viewpoint with a curious boat-like shelter. Continue on the waymarked path past the shelter for a good 250 yards to find a clear but unsigned cross path.

14 Turn left and follow this down to join a lane and continue right along this to a road junction in **Satterthwaite** by the church. Turn left back to the pub.

Place of interest nearby

Stott Park Bobbin Mill just north of Finsthwaite (follow the brown signs) was built in 1835 to produce the wooden bobbins vital to the Lancashire spinning and weaving industries. By diversifying into a wide variety of wooden items, from rungs for rope ladders used by the British Navy, to tool handles and toggles for duffle coats, the mill survived long after many others had closed down and Stott Park kept going until 1971. In 1983, the mill was reopened as a museum under the care of English Heritage. ☎ 015395 31087.

15 Lakeside

The Swan

This is an attractive short walk through woods and fields that can be combined with a ride on a steam train. It is ideal for children or a showery day when the walk can be done in a quick dash between raindrops. It is on quiet paths somewhat off the beaten track.

THE PUB

The **Swan** at Newby Bridge is a well-known Lake District establishment. The oldest part of the present building dates from 1623, before the bridge was built. The Georgian façade was added in 1766. Today it is a modern hotel with the Swan Inn at its core serving Cumbria Legendary Ales such as

The Lake District

Distance – 2 miles.

OS Explorer OL7 The English Lakes South-eastern area. GR SD 369863.

Starting point The Swan Hotel, Newby Bridge.

How to get there From the A590 at Newby Bridge, turn over the bridge to the Swan.

Alternatives The route described starts at Newby Bridge but there are several alternatives. One is to start at Haverthwaite station (large car park) on the A590, two miles west of Newby Bridge. Book a return ticket to Lakeside and get out at Newby Bridge Halt. Turn left out of the Halt and walk to the road junction by the Swan. Steam trains run from April to the end of October. (☎ 015395 31594 or www.lakesiderailway.co.uk). Another is to cruise on Windermere to Lakeside from Ambleside or Bowness (☎ 015394 32225 or www.windermere-lakescruises.co.uk) then catch the train to Newby Bridge Halt (or to Haverthwaite then back to Newby Bridge Halt) to start the walk. Combined cruise and train tickets are available. Finally, it is possible to do the walk without catching the train at all (see point 6).

the popular Loweswater Gold or why not try Dickie Doodle. The bar menu is attractive, including such favourites as a bacon butty (only in the morning), as well as other sandwiches, salads and main meals. The puddings are tempting, including Eton mess or scones with jam and clotted cream. There are tables outside on a terrace overlooking the River Leven.

Food is served all day, every day. ☎ 015395 31681; www.swanhotel.com.

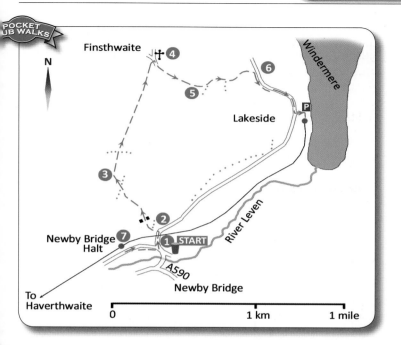

1 Turn right out of the **Swan** then right again at the road and walk over the railway bridge.

2 Immediately after the bridge turn left on a track signed 'Waterside Knott ½ mile Finsthwaite 1 mile'. Ignore a path on the right after 50 yards and continue on the track between buildings to a gate, then carry on along the woodland path ahead. Just over the brow of the hill go through a gap in a wall and continue on the main path to reach a stile on the right over a wall into a field.

3 Over the stile the path is not visible on the ground but goes more or less across the field to a squeeze stile at the far side. The

well-nourished walker may find it easier to go a few feet right to a gap in the wall. Continue in more or less the same direction across three further fields, with excellent views of the fells ahead. **Finsthwaite church** comes into view. Make straight for it across the fourth field to a gate onto a lane.

4 Turn right. After about 100 yards the surfaced lane ends. Go through a gate and continue in the same direction across two fields to a stile into a wood.

5 Follow the clear path through the wood ignoring two paths on the right.

6 Just before the road turn right on a track for a couple of hundred yards then turn left to the road. Turn right along the road to **Lakeside** to catch the train to **Newby Bridge**.

(If you do not wish to catch the train, continue along the road to Newby Bridge. There is a footpath on the right parallel with the road and signed 'Newby Bridge avoiding road' to reduce the amount of road walking.)

7 Get out at **Newby Bridge Halt**. Go to the road and turn left to the road junction at the **Swan Hotel**. There is a path parallel with the road on the bank of the **River Leven** for most of this.

Place of interest nearby

Lakes Aquarium at Lakeside features animals from the watery depths of the local lakes such as menacing pike and the iconic Arctic Char. An underwater tunnel enables visitors to appreciate a fish's eye view of a recreated Windermere lake bed. Lakes Aquarium is open every day from 9 am until 6 pm (5 pm in winter) ☎ 015395 30153; www.lakesaquarium.co.uk. If you definitely plan to visit the aquarium, a combined entry with a boat or train ticket offers a small saving.